WITHDRAWN

Bears

by Martin Schwabacher with Terry Miller Shannon

Marshall Cavendish
Benchmark
New York

Marshall Cavendish Benchmark
99 White Plains Road
Tarrytown, NY 10591
www.marshallcavendish.us

All websites were available and accurate when this book was sent to press.

Library of Congress Cataloging-in-Publication Data

Schwabacher, Martin.
   Bears / by Martin Schwabacher with Terry Miller Shannon.
     p. cm. – (Benchmark rockets. Animals)
   Includes bibliographical references and index.
   Summary: "Describes the physical characteristics, habitat, behavior, diet, life cycle, and conservation status of bears"–Provided by publisher.
   ISBN 978-0-7614-3820-5
1. Bears–Juvenile literature. I. Shannon, Terry Miller, 1951- II. Title.

QL737.C27S378 2010
599.78–dc22
2008051903

Publisher: Michelle Bisson
Editorial Development and Book Design: Trillium Publishing, Inc.

Photo research by Trillium Publishing, Inc.

Cover photo: Shutterstock.com/Rick Parsons

The photographs and illustrations in this book are used by permission and through the courtesy of: *Shutterstock.com:* nailat, 1; Richard Fitzer, 4–5; slowfish, 7 (top); Todd Pierson, 20; Thomas O'Neil, 21. *Alimidi. net:* Thomas Sbampato, 7 (bottom). *iStockphoto.com:* Erlend Kvalsvik, 8, 9; Thomas Pickard, 18; Frank van den Bergh, 19. *Marshall Cavendish Benchmark:* 10–11. *Spectrum Photofile:* 12–13. *Yukon Flats National Wildlife Refuge:* 14. *Corbis:* Kennan Ward, 16–17.

Printed in Malaysia
1 3 5 6 4 2

Contents

Brown bears, like this grizzly bear, are big and powerful.

Chapter 1

Bears of the World

Bears are **mammals**. They live in many different parts of the world. Some bears are small, like the sun bear. That bear is just a bit bigger than a dog. Other bears, like the polar bear, are very big.

Bears may look lazy and slow, but they are really strong and fast. They can bite through tree trunks and run faster than a horse. Some bears can run 40 miles (60 kilometers) an hour.

Most bears have short legs, small, round ears, and short tails. Their long claws help them climb trees and dig holes. Bears have a very good sense of smell.

5

There are eight kinds of bears. These bears have some of the same features. But each kind of bear looks a little bit different, too.

Brown bears are very large bears. They live in North America, Europe, and Asia. Their fur is not just brown but can be black, reddish, or blond.

Black bears also can have brown or reddish fur. They are smaller than brown bears. Black bears are the most common bears in North America.

Giant pandas have white and black fur and black patches around their eyes. They look cute and cuddly. Pandas live in China.

Sloth bears live in the mountains of South Asia. They have the longest fur of all bears. A baby sloth bear likes to hold onto its mother's fur and ride on her back.

A sloth bear (above) looks different from a spectacled bear (below).

Sun bears and moon bears also live in Asia. Moon bears have a white patch of fur shaped like a quarter-moon on their chests. Sun bears have a white or yellow patch on their chests. Sun bears spend most of the day in trees and hunt at night.

Spectacled bears live in the mountains of South America. They have white rings around their eyes that make them look like they are wearing glasses. These bears spend a lot of time in trees.

The bodies of polar bears help them live in the cold Arctic. Their white fur helps them hide in the snow. Their **webbed** front paws help them swim in icy water. Their fat helps them stay warm.

Bear Fact

Polar bears mostly eat seal and walrus meat. A polar bear can smell a seal from miles away. It can jump as far as 8 feet (2.4 meters) out of the water to grab a seal.

Most bears are **omnivores**. This means they eat both meat and plants. They like fruit, plant roots, bark, and grasses. Most bears eat insects and smaller animals like mice, lizards, and fish. Some bears eat larger animals such as deer or a farmer's goats or sheep. Bears like honey, too.

Sloth bears love to eat insects called **termites**. They use their long claws to dig termites out of termite nests.

Giant pandas are the only bears that do not eat meat at all. They only eat a plant called **bamboo**. Pandas eat up to 45 pounds (20.4 kilograms) of bamboo each day.

Bear Fact

Sun bears love to eat honey. Bees sting them, but these bears don't care. They eat the honey *and* the bees!

Kinds of Bears

Brown Bear

9 feet (2.7 m) long
425 pounds (192.8 kg)

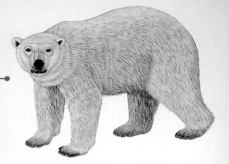

Polar Bear

8.5 feet (2.6 m) long
700 pounds (317.5 kg)

Giant Panda

6 feet (1.8 m) long
250 pounds (113 kg)

American Black Bear

5 feet (1.5 m) long
250 pounds (113 kg)

Asiatic Black Bear (Moon Bear)

5 feet (1.5 m) long
250 pounds (113 kg)

Sloth Bear

5 feet (1.5 m) long
250 pounds (113 kg)

Spectacled Bear

5 feet (1.5 m) long
250 pounds (113 kg)

Sun Bear

3 feet (0.9 m) long
80 pounds (36.3 kg)

Some bears, like this black bear, sleep through the winter in a den.

Chapter 2
Big Naps and Little Bears

For many bears, there is not much to eat when winter comes. These bears go into caves or **dens** in the fall and stay there until spring. They are **hibernating**.

Hibernating is like taking a very long nap. Bears do not eat anything while they are hibernating. Their hearts slow down. That way, they use less energy and they don't need to eat.

Bears that hibernate get ready for their long winter naps during the summer. They eat as much as they can. In one summer day, a brown bear may

13

eat 80 pounds (36 kg) of food. It may put on 3 to 6 pounds (1.4–2.7 kg) of fat.

Black bears hibernate longer the farther north they live. They want to get away from the cold. Black bears in Alaska may stay in their dens for up to seven months. Black bears in Mexico may sleep for just a few weeks because it's warmer there.

Not all bears hibernate. Polar bears don't hibernate. They hunt all year round. Sun bears and sloth bears don't hibernate, either, because they have lots of plants to eat all year round.

Even though not all bears hibernate, all female bears go into dens to have their **cubs**. Bear cubs' eyes are closed when they are born. A cub weighs less

Bear cubs, like these black bear cubs, are very small when they are born. Their eyes are closed.

than one pound (0.45 kg). Each tiny cub is small enough to hold in your hand.

The new cubs stay in the den for a few months. They drink their mother's milk. Safe in the den, they grow.

Two or three months pass. At last the cubs are big enough to come out of the den. The cubs stay close to their mother for two or three years. A mother bear and her cubs live by themselves, not with other bears.

Male cubs grow up to be big bears. They wrestle and fight each other. The winners get to mate with female bears. That way, the strong bears become fathers. The chances are that their cubs will be strong, too.

The father bears do not help the mother bears raise the cubs. Older male bears sometimes kill and eat the cubs. This is one of the dangers that cubs face.

Visitors to Alaska love to see the brown bears in the wild.

Chapter 3
Bears and People

Bears once were a danger to people and farm animals. This is still true in some places. But in most places, people have become a danger to bears. In fact, people are the biggest danger of all to bears.

People killed a lot of bears in the United States and Europe long ago. Brown bears are mostly gone from the United States. But brown bears still live in the northern parts of Canada and in Alaska.

The government of Alaska used to kill brown bears to help ranchers. The bears were killing their **livestock**. Now Alaska protects brown bears. People who visit Alaska want to see the bears.

Visitors spend a lot of money while they are in Alaska. This money is good for the state.

Polar bears are in danger because Earth is getting warmer. The ice in the Arctic Ocean is melting and polar bears are losing their hunting grounds. Polar bears need the ice to move from one place to another as they search for food. If polar bears are unable to find food, they will starve. If they have to swim a long way between blocks of ice, they may drown.

This polar bear and her cubs wait on a block of ice.

In many places around the world, more and more people are moving into bears' **habitats**. When that happens, bears don't have enough space to live. It becomes harder and harder for them to find enough food to eat.

This happened to giant pandas. They lost a lot of their habitat when people cut down bamboo forests to make farms and homes. Giant pandas need bamboo to live. Today there are only about 1,000 to 1,500 giant pandas left.

Many people are trying to save the giant panda. People have made paths between bamboo forests so that pandas can find enough bamboo to eat.

Without enough bamboo, pandas in the wild will die.

Many other bears are also losing their habitats. Spectacled bears in South America have trouble finding enough to eat because farmers are clearing the forests to make farms. The hungry bears sometimes kill livestock. Then the farmers kill the bears.

The habitats of the sun bear and the sloth bear are also getting smaller as people move in. There are fewer than 1,000 sloth bears alive today.

Some people think that the bones of a moon bear make good medicine.

Bears die when they lose their habitat. But they also die for other reasons. In Asia, some people kill bears for their body parts, such as bones or paws. They use the bear parts as charms or medicine. These people think the body parts will make them feel better.

People came up with a good plan to save black bears in Washington State. Black bears there were eating tree bark. One bear could kill 50 trees in one night. People wanted to save the trees, but they didn't want to kill the bears. Then they decided to leave bear food in the woods. The bears ate the food. They stopped eating the tree bark. This plan made both the bears and the people happy!

Sometimes people catch bears. They take them from their homes and put them in circuses.

Bears need people to help them **survive**. People who care about bears are fighting to make sure that enough land is saved for them. Other people are trying to stop the killing of bears for their body parts. But time is running out. If people do not do something now, bears may disappear from Earth forever.

21

Glossary

bamboo: A plant that grows in tropical places.

cubs: Young bears.

dens: Shelters or resting places of animals such as bears.

habitats: Places where plants or animals live or grow in nature.

hibernating: Spending the winter in a deep sleep.

livestock: Farm animals such as cows, sheep, and goats.

mammals: Warm-blooded animals that feed their young milk.

omnivores: Animals that eat both meat and plant foods.

survive: To continue to be alive.

termites: Ant-like bugs that eat wood.

webbed: Connected by a fold of skin.

Find Out More

Books

DK Publishing. *Bear.* New York: DK Children, 2003.

DK Publishing. *Panda.* New York: DK Children, 2008.

Kalman, Bobbie and Kylie Burns. *Endangered Bears.* New York: Crabtree Publishing Company, 2007.

Rosing, Norbert. *The World of the Polar Bear.* Buffalo, NY: Firefly Books, 2006.

Stefoff, Rebecca. *Bears* (AnimalWays). New York: Marshall Cavendish, 2002.

Stone, Lynn M. *Giant Pandas.* Minneapolis, MN: Lerner Publishing Group, 2004.

Websites

Cubs Corner: For Kids (The American Bear Association)
http://www.americanbear.org/Cubscorner.htm

National Geographic
http://animals.nationalgeographic.com/animals/mammals/spectacled-bear.html

http://animals.nationalgeographic.com/animals/mammals/giant-panda.html

http://animals.nationalgeographic.com/animals/mammals/sloth-bear.html

North American Bear Center
http://www.bear.org

San Diego Zoo
http://www.sandiegozoo.org/animalbytes/t-sun_bear.html

Index

Page numbers for photographs and illustrations are in **boldface**.